# MODERN ARNIS

by Remy Presas

## THE FILIPINO ART OF STICK FIGHTING

**Editor: Gregory Lee**
**Graphic Design: Karen Massad**

**Art Production: Mary Schepis**

© 1983 Ohara Publications, Inc.
All rights reserved
Printed in the United States of America
Library of Congress Catalog Card Number 83-60128
ISBN: 0-89750-089-X

*Twentieth printing 2003*

### WARNING

OHARA ▮ PUBLICATIONS, INCORPORATED
SANTA CLARITA, CALIFORNIA

## ACKNOWLEDGEMENTS

I wish to thank my excellent students who assisted me in the techniques photographed for this book: Jeffrey Arnold, Dan DiVito, Michael Replogle, Roland Roemer, Jr., and Tom Zoppi. My appreciation also to our patient photographer, Marcia Mack.

R.P.

Thanks to Michael for his invaluable assistance in the preparation of this manuscript—your contributions made the difference.

G.L.

## ABOUT THE AUTHOR

Remy Amador Presas is one of the most vibrant personalities in the martial arts. One of the Philippines' premier stick fighters, Presas has become a national figure in his native country for his blending of the countless island combat styles into one system, which he named Modern Arnis.

Presas began his study of arnis at an early age, leaving home at 14 to pursue his interest in the fighting arts characteristic of his homeland. Presas ultimately synthesized important aspects from *kali, escrima, tjakalele* and *arnis de mano* into the art he teaches today. His travel throughout the Philippines led to the rise of arnis as a national sport, taught regularly in physical education classes throughout the country.

Presas left the Philippines in 1975 on a goodwill tour sponsored by the Philippine government to spread arnis to other countries. He arrived in the United States, conducting special seminars to groups as diverse as law enforcement agencies and senior citizens. The "Professor" (as his students affectionately call him) has been welcomed wherever he goes, demonstrating the daring techniques of the *bolo* and the bewitching twirl of double rattan sticks—the *sinawali*.

In 1982, Presas was inducted into the *Black Belt* Hall of Fame as Instructor of the Year for his devotion to teaching the art he loves. Years of refinement have given Presas a personal style that makes his seminars among the most popular at many martial art schools.

Presas currently resides in San Francisco, and he is actively involved with the formation of his International Arnis Federation (IAF), headquartered in Los Angeles.

Readers who are interested in furthering their studies in the art of arnis, or who have comments or questions about this book, are encouraged to write to IAF at 124 Rolph St., San Francisco, CA 94112.

# HISTORY

The origins of *arnis* are difficult to trace, primarily because there are nearly as many styles of Filipino stick fighting as their are islands in the Philippine archipelago—more than 7,000! The races that settled in these islands came from India, Southeast Asia, China and Indonesia.

These diverse races and cultures blended their heritages over the centuries, producing a common method for employing sharp swords, daggers and fire-hardened sticks in combat. These highly sophisticated fighting styles have grown in popularity in the international martial arts community.

One of the earliest known forms was called *tjakalele*, (Indonesian fencing). *Kali* is another term familiar to stick fighters around the world today.

When the Philippines were invaded by the Spanish, the invaders required guns to subdue their fierce opponents. The deadly fighting skills of Filipino warriors nearly overwhelmed them, and they dubbed the native stick style *escrima* (skirmish). Escrima was subsequently outlawed, but the techniques did not disappear. They were preserved in secret, sometimes under the very noses of the conquerors, in the form of dances or mock battles staged in religious plays known as *moro-moro*.

These plays featured Filipinos, sometimes costumed as Spanish soldiers wearing *arnes*, the harnesses worn during medieval times for armor. The blade fighting forms and footwork were identical to those used in escrima. The word arnes soon became corrupted to *arnis*, and the name stuck.

Historically, arnis incorporated three related methods: *espada y daga* (sword and dagger), which employs a long blade and a short dagger; *solo baston* (single stick); and *sinawali* (to weave), which uses two sticks of equal length, twirled in "weaving" fashion for blocking and striking (the term derives from *sinawali*, the bamboo matting woven in the Philippines).

When Remy Amador Presas first traveled his country, he took what he considered to be the most effective principles of each island style and combined them with his own knowledge of other martial arts, such as karate, judo and kenpo. Modern Arnis, as Presas terms his system, incorporates empty hand moves based upon the same motions used in solo baston and sinawali. Unlike kali, his system also uses low kicks and takedowns for a more well-rounded approach.

Presas also insisted on modernizing a particular training aspect traditional in arnis: that of hitting your opponent's hand or arm instead of his stick—a painful practice that was tolerated because the rattan canes used in arnis were considered sacred. Presas decided that hitting the stick was just as good a practice method and would obviously discourage far fewer students of arnis, preventing many painful injuries.

Presas does not merely combine techniques—he encourages the individual student to adapt arnis principles to his own feel for each technique. The method should suit the person and not the other way around. This is known simply as using "the flow." The flow is Presas' universal term for defining the comfortable place where the movements of arnis and the individual human body meet for maximum effectiveness; body and weapon blend to achieve the most natural fighting style based on an individual's needs and attitudes.

"Arnis makes many martial artists discover new things about their own style," says Presas. "They recognize the beauty of arnis because it blends naturally the best movements from many arts. Most of my students continue to study their own styles—they just use arnis to supplement their understanding."

For his seminars, Presas has further simplified some of his teaching in order to give novices a tangible amount of self-defense skill through specific drills. Sinawali, for instance, is practiced first with the hands in "patty cake" fashion, then the sticks are picked up and the student repeats these motions.

Presas demonstrates how these weaving motions can be translated into empty hand movements for blocking, punching and takedowns. He has designated 12 important angles of attack on the human body, and 12 basic ways of dealing with each angle. There are also many disarming techniques (demonstrated in this book), and the variations and improvisational capabilities implied are endless.

Arnis is a growing art, expanding in this country rapidly. Arnis tends to transcend stylistic distinctions, and discovery seems to be a primary benefit from the study of Modern Arnis, especially under the methods of Remy Presas.

# CONTENTS

# CHAPTER 1

# Warm-Ups

**T**he need for basic warm-up, muscle-building and limbering exercises prior to any training, in the martial arts or any athletic endeavor, is obvious. The exercises depicted here are only a sampling of those I employ in a typical class for Modern Arnis. Other basic workout routines, including isometric exercises, aerobics (such as running and jumping rope), stretching, weight training and other forms, are all recommended for keeping the body fit for arnis practice.

Try these exercises as part of your introductory training, and be sure to use them daily. Do several repetitions of each exercise.

### WINDMILLS

(1) Stand straight with your feet approximately shoulder-width apart, trunk straight ahead and your arms spread outward, palms down. (2) Begin twisting your upper body at the waist, first to the left, bringing your right arm around to your left as you move your left arm back and to your right. Now twist back (3) in the opposite direction and repeat. Go back and forth ten or 20 times.

### KNEE LIFTS

(1) Stand straight with your heels close together and your arms loosely at your sides. (2) Pick your left knee up, grasping your shin with your left hand and assisting your knee all the way up until you can touch your chest. (3) Repeat with the right knee. Do a set of ten or 20.

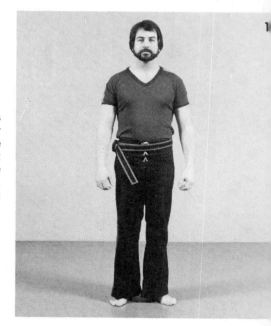

## TRUNK STRETCH

(1) Stand straight with your feet approximately shoulder-width apart,
your arms raised high over your head.
(2-4) Begin bending at the waist and
swing your upper torso down to the
right in an arc until you are bent forward near the ground. (5&6) Now bend
back up and to your left in an arc until
you return to the starting position.
Now repeat in the opposite direction.

2

3

5

6

13

## PALM-TO-FLOOR

This is a variation on the old toe-touching exercise. (1) Stand straight with your feet approximately two shoulder-widths apart and your arms spread at your sides, palms out. (2) Bend at the waist and bring your right arm down, touching the ground in front of your left foot with your palm. Bring your left arm back behind your head. (3) Repeat on the opposite side, left palm toward right foot. Do 20 repetitions.

## ARM ROTATIONS

This is for loosening up the muscles in the wrists and arms, particularly important in arnis. (1) Stand straight with feet spread comfortably apart and your arms spread wide at your sides grasping a cane in each hand, palms forward. (2&3) Twist your arms forward and then back, stopping when the sticks are parallel to the ground and then reversing the direction, back and forth. To make the exercise more difficult, grasp each stick near one end.

## ARM CIRCLES

(1) Stand straight with your feet spread comfortably apart and your arms at your sides. (2-5) Swing your arms simultaneously in front of you, then over your head and back behind you in a 360-degree arc. Swing them backward several times, then stop and swing them forward for several repetitions.

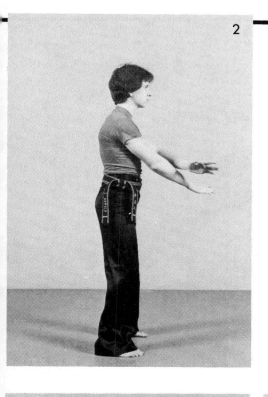

## PUSH-UPS

(1) Position your body above the floor with your palms flat supporting most of your weight and your knees off the ground, legs on tiptoes. (2) Lower your body until your chin is close to the ground in standard push-up fashion. (3) Vary the push-up exer-

cise by first raising your hips while keeping your chin low to the ground, then (4) lower your hips as you straighten your elbows and raise only your head away from the ground. Repeat.

# CHAPTER 2

# Preparations

There are only a few specific stances or ready positions in Modern Arnis, but learning them is essential before they become a part of your automatic response in a self-defense situation. Effective balance and the ability to move swiftly backward and forward to facilitate blocking and striking are the backbone of arnis or any martial art.

Stances or ready positions are not static things to be assumed and then maintained throughout practice. The body flows into each appropriate stance as the situation demands. The first few postures shown here are formal stances and the assumed ready positions are prepatory to starting each practice session.

Also included in this section is the formal courtesy of Modern Arnis, performed at the beginning and end of any practice, and the proper way to hold the traditional cane or stick.

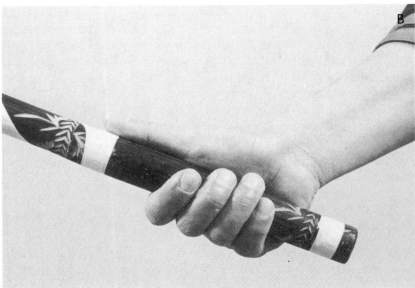

## THE GRIP

To grasp the arnis stick properly, hold it firmly as if shaking hands (A) and fold your thumb on top of your first finger. Do not leave the thumb exposed (B) on top of the stick, as this may cause injury. Keep the wrist relaxed.

## ATTENTION STANCE

(A) The closed attention stance is assumed during the courtesy, before any practice session and at the end of a practice session. Your heels are together, feet pointed outward at a 45-degree angle. The stick is held horizontally with your arms relaxed on either side. Your eyes are focused straight ahead. (B) The open attention stance is identical to the closed stance, except that your feet are spread approximately shoulder width apart.

---

## OPEN LEG READY STANCE

This stance is assumed in preparation for a direct frontal assault. The legs are in the same position as the informal attention stance, but the knees are slightly bent and the stick is now held out with the right hand (at a 45-degree angle respective to the ground) and the left hand is held directly behind it to guard, or support a block.

**FRONT VIEW** — **SIDE VIEW**

23

FRONT
VIEW

SIDE
VIEW

## STRADDLE STANCE

Similar to the open leg ready stance, but the legs are spread further apart, approximately two shoulder widths and the knees bent further. The stick and opposite hand are in the same position as the open leg ready position.

## RIGHT FORWARD STANCE

In this stance, the right foot is planted forward and the weight distributed evenly on both feet. The stick and opposite hand are still held up in the ready position. The left forward position is assumed by stepping forward with the left leg. Your trunk remains facing forward.

FRONT
VIEW

SIDE
VIEW

**FRONT VIEW**

**SIDE VIEW**

## RIGHT BACK STANCE

The weight is now shifted slightly to the rear foot, about 60 percent on your rear foot and 40 percent on your front foot. The feet are now forming an L-shape with the toes of the back foot pointing 90 degrees to the left. The stick and hand remain in the same ready position. The left back stance is assumed by stepping forward with the left leg.

## OBLIQUE FORWARD STANCE

Similar to the forward stance except that the trunk is now twisted 45 degrees to the right or left of the forward stance to face an assault from another direction. The front knee is bent deeper and more weight is on the forward foot. Both heels and toes remain planted firmly on the ground. The hands and stick remain in the same ready position.

**LEFT**

**RIGHT**

# BODY SHIFTING

Learning to employ body shifting in arnis is extremely important. Virtually all the techniques in this book employ some degree of body shifting to move

## EXAMPLE #1

(1) You and your opponent are about five feet apart. When your opponent moves in with a backhand strike (2) you should step forward at a 45-degree angle (with your left foot) and block, closing the distance. Inset 2A shows how to shift if attacked with a forehand strike.

your body away from the opponent's angle of attack, yet close the distance so that an effective defense can be used (counterstrike, disarm, takedown).

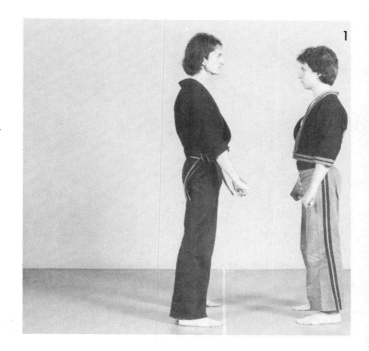

**EXAMPLE #2**

(1) If you are too close to your opponent, when he steps in with a backhand strike (2) you should step back 45 degrees (with your right foot) in order to maintain a working distance from him while still avoiding the angle of his attack. Inset 2B shows how to shift if attacked with a forehand strike.

## THE COURTESY

This is the official modern arnis salute. (1) Face your partner/opponent with your feet together, body erect, holding your stick parallel to the ground in both hands (palms down). (2) Move your left foot until your feet are shoulder width apart in an open leg stance. (3) Bring your left

foot back and raise your stick up in your right hand so that it is perpendicular to the ground, and bring your left hand up, palm flat against your chest. (4) Return to the open leg stance with your stick held horizontally in both hands (the same as step 2).

# CHAPTER 3

# The 12-Zone Striking System

**T**he 12 angles of attack in Modern Arnis are both a way of memorizing the major, vital areas of the body that can be attacked, and also a sequence of strikes practiced as a drill in a specific order to familiarize the student with the 12 basic strikes.

The 12 vital areas are: the left and right temples, the left and right shoulders, the stomach or groin, the left and right sides of the chest, the knees, the eyes and the crown of the head. Stick strikes to any of these areas are all injurious, many fatal.

The arnis student learns the strikes in a prescribed sequence and practices striking to these areas over and over in order to understand the angles of attack in approaching these zones, and how an opponent's approach often telegraphs his own intended target area.

The numbered zones are referred to throughout the book for reference; when showing a defense, the text may say, "The attacker attempts a strike to #2 . . ." The technique will then illustrate how to counter such an attack. Learn these 12 strikes, both as a point of reference for defending your own body and for striking the target areas of your opponent.

The following striking drill is practiced as one continuous sequence, though the 12 strikes are also broken down here individually for easier instruction. Notice that your body will shift almost automatically into the proper stances as you execute each strike. Though the instructions are shown for the right hand only, you should practice the left hand equally, mirroring the movements of the right hand.

# THE 12-ZONE
# STRIKING DRILL
## (At a glance)

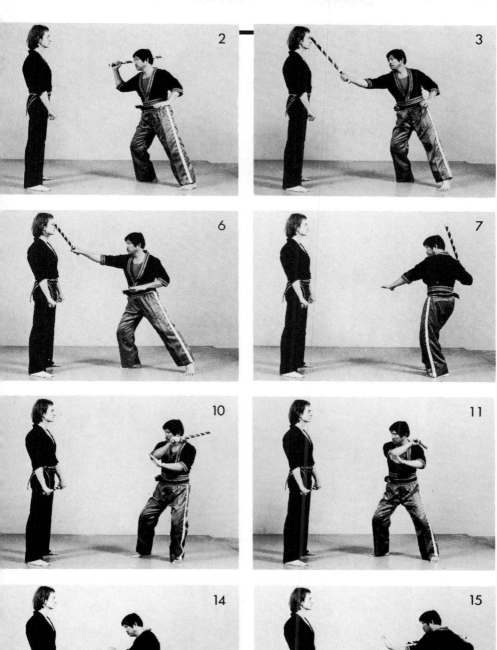

Continued on next page

16

17

20

21

24

25

28

29

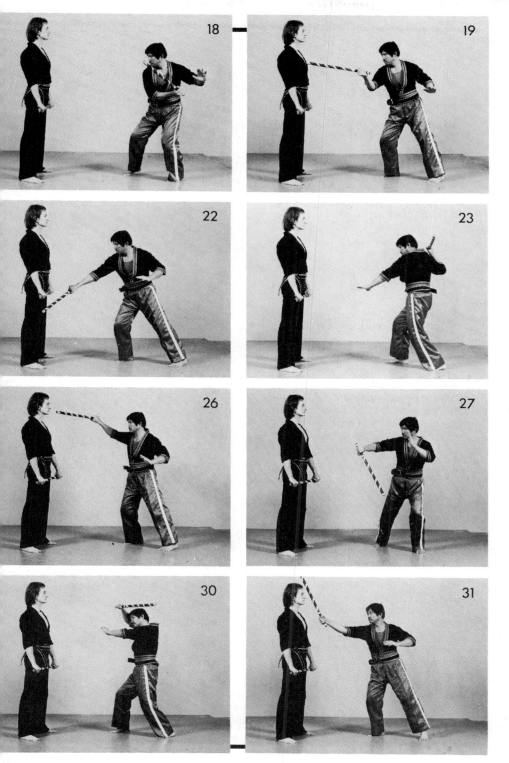

### STRIKE #1

From the ready position, (1) step in with your right foot while drawing your right hand back toward the right side of your head and (2) execute a forehand strike to your opponent's left temple, following through (3) in one continuous motion by drawing your stick back to the left side of your head, ready for Strike #2.

### STRIKE #2

Starting from the final position of Strike #1, (1) step in with your right foot while drawing your stick hand behind your head for a backhand strike (2) to your opponent's right temple, following through (3) by drawing your stick all the way back to the right side of your body, ready for Strike #3.

### STRIKE #3

Starting from the final position of Strike #2, (1) step in with your right foot while drawing your stick back and execute a forehand strike (2) to your opponent's left side, following through (3) by drawing your stick across to the left side of your body, ready for Strike #4.

2

3

2

3

2

3

## STRIKE #4

Starting from the final position of Strike #3, (1) step in with your right foot while drawing your stick back and execute a backhand strike (2) to your opponent's right side, following through (3) by drawing your stick straight back to the right side of your waist, ready for Strike #5.

## STRIKE #5

Starting from the final position of Strike #4, (1) step in with your right foot and execute a forehand thrust (2) straight into your opponent's solar plexus. Withdraw the stick (3) back to the same side of your body while raising your right arm and elbow, ready for Strike #6.

## STRIKE #6

Starting from the final position of Strike #5, (1) step in with your right foot and execute a forehand thrust (2) straight to the left side of your opponent's chest, following through (3) by dipping the end of your stick down in a clockwise arc past your left knee, ready for Strike #7.

2

3

2

3

2

3

### STRIKE #7

Starting from the final position of Strike #6, (1) continue the arcing motion from Strike #6, lifting your stick in a clockwise circle past your left shoulder as you step in and execute a (2) backhand thrust to the right side of your opponent's chest, withdrawing your stick (3) back the way it came to the left side of your body, ready for Strike #8.

### STRIKE #8

Starting from the final position of Strike #7, (1) step in with your right foot while drawing your stick back counterclockwise and execute a backhand strike (2) to your opponent's right knee, following through (3) by drawing your stick across to the right side of your body, ready for Strike #9.

### STRIKE #9

Starting from the final position of Strike #8, (1) step in with your right foot while drawing your stick back and execute a forehand strike (2) to your opponent's left knee, following through (3) and drawing your stick straight back to the right side of your head, ready for Strike #10.

2

3

2

3

2

3

### STRIKE #10

Starting from the final position of Strike #9, (1) step in while raising your stick high on your right side and execute a forehand thrust (2) straight to your opponent's left eye, following through (3) by dipping the end of your stick down in a clockwise arc past your left knee, ready for Strike #11.

### STRIKE #11

Starting from the final position of Strike #10, (1) continue the clockwise arcing motion from Strike #10, lifting the stick in a circle past your left shoulder and executing a (2) backhand thrust to your opponent's right eye, withdrawing your stick (3) counterclockwise above your head, ready for Strike #12.

### STRIKE #12

Starting from the final position of Strike #11, (1) continue circling your stick counterclockwise above your head and step in to strike (2) downward directly on top of your opponent's head, following through (3) by bringing your stick back to the ready position.

# CHAPTER 4

# The 12-Zone Striking Defenses

**T**he following are some of the basic defenses used against the 12 major strikes. Though they are broken down carefully in these photographs, they are meant to be executed in one smooth and swift motion, with no distinct pauses between the block, check and counterstrike motions.

Keep in mind that when blocking one stick with your own, your free hand should always be poised to guard, ready to brace a stick block or grab an opponent's stick. You must stay loose and move quickly, always pivoting to face the strike and keep your balance.

There are many variations in arnis on the defenses shown here— these are only the most basic. A stick-versus-stick situation is illustrated, followed each time with the same identical motions of defense performed empty-handed against the same stick attack. The beauty of arnis is in the translation from stick defense to empty hand defense with no major modifications in reaction. This helps accelerate a student's training in arnis, since he or she can learn both forms in practice at the same time, and see the correlation between the two.

Although in most of the following illustrations the stick strikes (and blocks) the opponent's stick, in actual combat you would strike the opponent's wrist, forearm or elbow. In practice, you *always* block the opponent's stick, *never* his arm.

### DEFENSE AGAINST
### STRIKES #1 OR #3

(1) As your opponent steps in with a forehand strike to the left side of your body (Strikes #1 or #3), sidestep to your right (2) to avoid his strike as you execute an outside block, using your left hand to check (3) his right hand. Draw your stick back underneath your left arm and strike (4) swiftly to your opponent's chest or stomach.

**1**

## UNARMED DEFENSE
## AGAINST STRIKES #1 OR #3

(1) As your opponent attempts a forehand strike to the left side of your body, (2) sidestep to your right as you deflect his strike with your right hand. (3) Check his right hand with your left hand and (4) strike your opponent's solar plexus or groin with your right hand.

**2**

**3**

**4**

## DEFENSE AGAINST
## STRIKES #2 OR #4

(1) As your opponent threatens with a backhand strike to the right side of your body (Strikes #2 or #4), sidestep (2) to your left to avoid his strike as you swing your right stick out to execute an inside block. Follow immediately (3) with a left hand check (and/or grab) and (4) execute a strike to his left temple (Strike #1).

1

## UNARMED DEFENSE
## AGAINST STRIKES #2 OR #4

(1) As your opponent attempts a back-hand strike to the right side of your body, (2) sidestep to your left to avoid the strike as you block his right hand with your left hand, sweeping your left hand underneath your right arm as you check (3) his right hand with your right hand. (4) Grip his right hand as you strike your opponent's groin with your left hand.

*Note:* In this case, the defender initiated the block with his left hand instead of his right, as shown in the example on the opposite page.

2

3

4

### DEFENSE AGAINST
### STRIKE #5

(1) As your opponent attempts a fore-hand thrust to your midsection (Strike #5), (2) sidestep to your right to avoid the thrust while executing a vertical block (tip of your stick pointing at the ground), checking (3) with your left hand as you draw your stick underneath your left arm and immediately strike (4) your opponent's groin or solar plexus.

## UNARMED DEFENSE
## AGAINST STRIKE #5

(1) As your opponent attempts a forehand thrust to your midsection, (2) sidestep to your right to avoid his thrust as you block his right hand with your right hand. Check (3) his right hand with your left hand as you draw your right hand back for a strike (4) to your opponent's groin.

## DEFENSE AGAINST
## STRIKES #6 OR #10

(1) As your opponent attempts a fore-hand thrust to the left side of your body or head (Strikes #6 or #10), (2) sidestep to your right as you execute an outside block with your stick. (3) Check his right hand with your left hand as you draw your stick back underneath your left arm and strike (4) your opponent's ribs.

## UNARMED DEFENSE
## AGAINST STRIKES #6 OR #10

(1) As your opponent attempts a fore-hand thrust to the left side of your body or head, (2) sidestep to your right as you parry his right hand with your right hand. (3) Check his right hand with your left hand as you draw your right hand underneath your left arm and strike (4) your opponent's ribs.

## DEFENSE AGAINST
## STRIKES #7 OR #11

(1) As your opponent attempts a backhand thrust to the right side of your body or head (Strikes #7 or #11), (2) sidestep to your left as you execute an inside block. (3) Check your opponent's right hand with your left hand as you raise your stick high and (4) execute a strike to your opponent's left temple (Strike #1).

## UNARMED DEFENSE
## AGAINST STRIKES #7 OR #11

(1) As your opponent attempts a back-hand thrust to the right side of your body or head, (2) sidestep to your left as you block with your left hand. (3) Check his right hand with your right hand as you raise your left hand for a strike (4) to your opponent's head.
*Note*: Here again, the hand initiating the block varies with stick or empty-hand situations.

## DEFENSE AGAINST STRIKE #8

(1) As your opponent attempts a low backhand strike to the right side of your body (Strike #8), (2) sidestep to your left as you raise your stick high to the left side of your body and execute a strike (3) to the outside of your opponent's right wrist or forearm.

*Note:* In practice, you *never* strike your partner's body—only his stick.

## DEFENSE AGAINST STRIKE #9

(1) As your opponent attempts a low forehand strike to the left side of your body (Strike #9), (2) sidestep to your right as you raise your stick on the right side of your body and execute a strike (3) to the inside of your opponent's right wrist or forearm.

*Note:* In practice, you *never* strike your partner's body—only his stick.

## UNARMED DEFENSE
## AGAINST STRIKE #8

(1) As your opponent attempts a low backhand strike to the right side of your body, (2) sidestep to your left as you block his right hand with your right hand. (3) Check with your left hand on his right arm as you draw your right hand back and execute a strike (4) to your opponent's head.

## UNARMED DEFENSE AGAINST STRIKE #9

(1) As your opponent attempts a low forehand strike to the left side of your body, (2) sidestep to your right as you block with your right hand. (3) Check your opponent's right wrist with your left hand as you raise your right hand high to strike (4) your opponent's head.

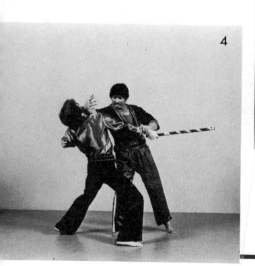

## DEFENSE AGAINST STRIKE #12

(1) As your opponent attempts a downward strike to your head (Strike #12), sidestep to your right (2&3) as you execute a slashing strike upward across your opponent's right arm and follow immediately with a check to his right wrist with your left hand. (4) Grab the wrist and pull your opponent off balance, executing a strike to his left temple (Strike #1).

## UNARMED DEFENSE AGAINST STRIKE #12

(1) As your opponent attempts a downward strike to your head, sidestep to your right (2&3) and execute a two-hand upward block and deflect your opponent's right wrist with your left hand. Raise your right hand high and execute a strike (4) to his head.

# CHAPTER 5

# Trapping Hands

**T**his section illustrates hand-to-hand combat using the same basic defense patterns shown previously, with or without a stick. Each example (whether inside vs. outside, left vs. right) is followed by a close-up of the same action for a better understanding of the rolling and trading-off action of the hands. Note that the striking surface, whether back fist or just knuckles, is not as important as quickly parrying the potential punch, checking the attacker's arm out of the way and delivering the counterstrike.

Also included is the *de cadena* (of chains), an exercise in trading off hands with a partner to practice the flow and to increase speed and agility. Another purpose of many arnis drills is to get the student comfortable with reacting instantaneously with either hand, to the inside or outside, without any difference in response or ability.

## INSIDE DEFENSE
### (vs. Right Punch)

(1&2) As your opponent attempts a right punch, shift to your right and parry with your right hand (3) by executing a brushing block to his right wrist. (4) As you reach up with your left hand to check (and/or grab) his right wrist, draw your

right hand up from under your left elbow and (5) execute a backhand strike to your opponent's head. You can add more to the impact of the blow by yanking on your opponent's right wrist, pulling him into the strike.

## CLOSE-UP OF INSIDE DEFENSE
### (vs. Right Punch)

(1&2) Parry and shift simultaneously to brush block a right punch, drawing your left hand up (3&4) to check (and/or grab) his wrist while

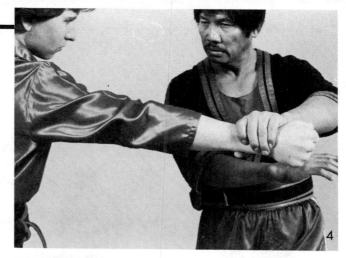

freeing your right hand again (5&6) to deliver the counterstrike to your opponent's head.

## INSIDE DEFENSE
### (vs. Left Punch)

(1&2) As your opponent steps in with a left punch, shift to your left as you parry his strike to your right with your left hand using a brush block on the in-

side of his left wrist and (3&4) quickly checking (and/or grabbing) with your right hand. Use your left hand for a (5) backhand strike to his head.

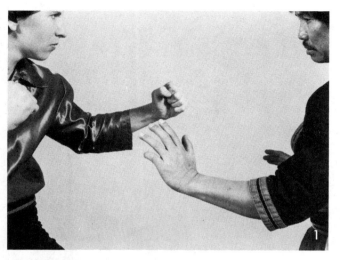

### CLOSE-UP OF
### INSIDE DEFENSE
**(vs. Left Punch)**

(1&2) Parry your opponent's left punch by brush blocking left-to-right with your left hand, (3) drawing your right hand up to check (and/or grab) his left wrist while (4&5) freeing your left

hand again to deliver a backhand strike to your opponent's head. Your left hand and arm are also in a position to block a possible counterstrike by your opponent.

## OUTSIDE DEFENSE
### (vs. Right Punch)

The identical motions are employed whether blocking an opponent's punch to the outside or the inside. (1&2) As your opponent attempts a right punch, shift to your left as you block and parry his punch using your left hand on the outside of his right wrist. (3) Continue shoving his right arm, binding up his potential left counter in the pro-

cess, and trade hands (4), checking (and/or grabbing) with your right hand and freeing your left hand for a backhand strike (5) to your opponent's head. Notice the change in position relative to your opponent by shifting to the outside instead of the inside, creating many possible angles of counterattack.

## CLOSE-UP OF OUTSIDE DEFENSE
### (vs. Right Punch)

(1&2) When your opponent attempts a right punch, brush block on the outside of his right wrist from left to right, (3&4) then check

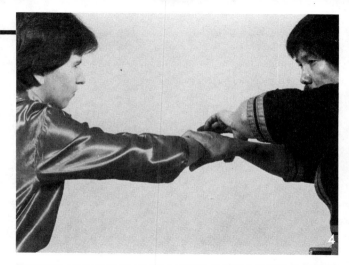

with your right hand by grabbing his right wrist and pulling, freeing your left hand (5&6) for the counterstrike to his head.

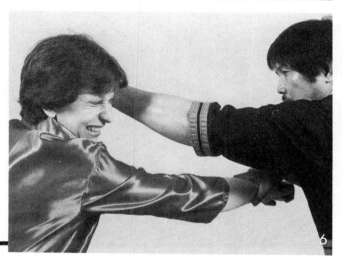

## OUTSIDE DEFENSE
### (vs. Left Punch)

(1&2) As your opponent steps in with a left punch, shift to your right outside his punch, brush blocking across your body with your right hand, then checking (and/or grabbing) (3) with

your left hand as you draw
your right hand back under
your elbow, (4&5) coun-
tering with a backhand
strike to your opponent's
head.

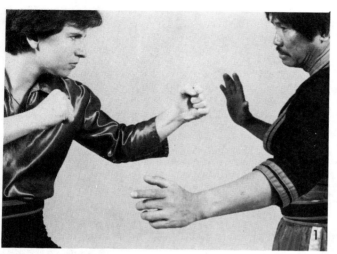

**CLOSE-UP OF
OUTSIDE DEFENSE
(vs. Left Punch)**

(1&2) As your opponent attempts a left punch, parry from right to left with your right hand on the back of your opponent's left wrist, then (3) check (and/or grab)

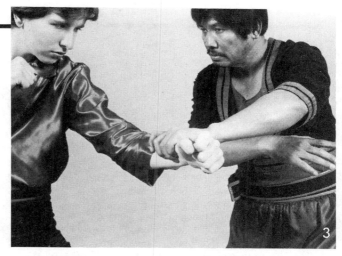

with your left hand on his wrist and draw your right hand back (4&5) to deliver a counterstrike to your opponent's head.

## DE CADENA

(1) Throw a right punch to your partner's head, which he will brush block inside with his right hand (2) and check with his left. Your partner counters with a right backhand strike (3) to your head, which you will parry (4) from the outside with your left hand. (5) Check with your right hand and throw a backfist (6) to his head. (7&8) He will parry your strike to the outside with his left hand and attempt to counter with a right backhand strike (9) to your head. (10) Counter his strike with an inside brush block, using your right hand to brush from right to left and checking (11) with your left hand. Counter (12) with another right backfist to his head which he parries (13) to the outside with his left hand, and so forth.

# CHAPTER 6

# Flow Practice

**T**he flow exercises that follow are for partners, and are performed both with sticks and with empty hands. These will familiarize you with the flow, the way your body and hands can weave in and out of an attack to convert your opponent's momentum into an opening that you can exploit. These drills should be a regular part of your arnis training, and the speed at which you can perform them should gradually increase with experience. But for the moment, practice them in virtual slow motion and feel "the flow."

Though the following drills (and many in this book) depict a right-handed approach, all drills should be practiced as much or more using your left hand. This is crucial to mastering arnis.

In the following drill, one partner will slowly attack using just one stick while the other person defends by using a series of parry-and-slash motions. Your stick hand and free hand criss-cross continually in front of your body as you deflect an opponent's strike *into* your counter-strike. Imagine that your stick is a sword and that you are "slicing" your opponent's arm.

## FLOW PRACTICE
### (with Sticks)

(1) As your partner (pictured here on the left) steps in with a low forehand strike (Strike #9), sidestep to your right (2) and parry his stick from your left to your right with your free hand while using your stick to "slice" the inside of his stick arm. (3) Follow through, bringing your stick all the way across your body and continue pushing his stick away. (4-6) As he counters with a low backhand strike (Strike #8), use a backhand strike on the outside of his stick arm and parry his stick with your free hand from right to left, always deflecting and striking simultaneously. (7-9) If your opponent tries an overhead strike (Strike #12), duck low and to your right and use a forehand strike across the inside of his stick arm as you deflect with your free hand from left to right. Be sure to bring your stick all the way across preparing for his next attack. (10-12) As he counters with a high backhand strike (Strike #2), strike the outside of his stick arm with a backhand strike and use your free hand to brush his stick hand away from right to left. Continue this drill, back and forth, slowly increasing the speed of attack.

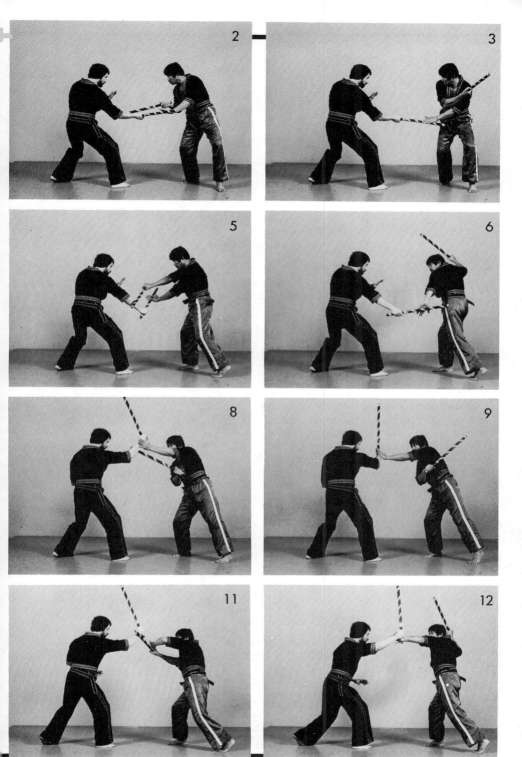

## FLOW PRACTICE
### (with Hands)

This drill is similar to the previous one, except that the defender uses only his hands to parry and "slice" his attacker's stick arm. (1-4) When your partner attacks with a low forehand strike, brush the inside of his stick arm with your right hand as you parry his stick with your left hand. (5-9) As he tries a low backhand strike, use your left hand to pull his stick from right to left while striking his right arm with your right hand. Continue to push his

2

4

5

7

Continued on next page

8

stick away. (10-13) As he counters with an overhead forehand strike, push his stick hand from left to right with your left hand and cut the inside of his right wrist with your right hand, always keeping low to avoid his attack. (14&15) As he tries an overhead backhand strike, parry his stick hand from right to left with your left hand, simultaneously slicing his forearm from left to right with your right hand. Follow this same procedure continuously, always parrying and slicing in the same motion. Flow easily from one strike to the next without stopping and let your partner gradually increase the speed of his attacks. Notice that you never try to stop a strike with a block, but always permit the strike to flow past you in the same direction.

10

13

9

11

12

14

15

## COMBINED GIVE AND TAKE DRILL

This exercise combines elements of both the flow practice and the 12 strikes. Partners alternately attack and defend, converting their defensive blocks and flowing into their next attack. In this hypothetical example, (1&2) one partner steps in and executes a #3 strike, which the other person blocks and checks using an outside block (3) and then follows (4&5) with a low backhand strike. The first man (6) blocks the opponent's right hand with his left as he slices down on top of the opponent's stick (7), then raises his stick high (8&9) for an overhead strike (Strike #12). His opponent uses the flow to parry the opponent's stick to the outside (10&11) while

2

3

5

6

9

10

Continued on next page

slashing across his opponent's stick from left to right. (12&13) The first man executes an outside block to parry his opponent's forehand strike, checking with his left hand and attempting a low backhand strike (14) to his opponent's ribs. (15-17) The opponent blocks the first man's right hand downward with his left hand and slices his opponent's stick, countering with a high overhead strike. (18) The first man parries his opponent's stick hand to the left and slices across with his right. (19&20) His next move is a forehand strike, which his opponent checks with an outside block. The sequence can go on continuously in any direction.

12

13

15

16

19

20

# CHAPTER 7

# The Sinawali and Redonda

**S**inawali are weaving motions made with two sticks in Arnis that are practiced in precise, prescribed motions to familiarize the student with the method of stick fighting, both in free sparring and with blades.

There are three basic types of sinawali in Arnis: the single sinawali, the double sinawali and the reverse sinawali. All employ two sticks (or two hands) and can be practiced with a partner. Both partners employ the same motions, up and down, left to right, at the same time. As you practice each sinawali, you should make firm contact with your partner's cane or stick, and not be afraid to make some honest noise. Your wrists, forearms and shoulders will soon feel new dexterity as you practice sinawali over and over. It is both a fine exercise for the upper body and arms as well as good programming for learning to defend against another's stick or blade.

The sinawali are also taught without the sticks, in empty hand fashion, to illustrate how the sinawali motions can be easily translated for empty hand defense. The weaponless defender can use the sinawali motion to fend off an attacker who is armed with a cane or blade. The application in defense with empty hands will be shown after each sinawali exercise is illustrated.

The variations of sinawali are numerous, but the three outlined here are the basis of the Arnis system.

The hand versions of each sinawali are shown first, which will make your subsequent practice with the sticks easier.

## SINGLE SINAWALI
### (Hands)

(1) In the ready position, your right hand is held high near your right ear, and your left arm is bent so that your forearm is parallel to the ground and your left palm is near your waist. (2) Both men slap their right palms together midway between them and follow through (3&4) without stopping as they lower their right palms to slap in a low position. Your hands meet by moving your right arm counterclockwise. At the same time that your right hands meet in the lower position, raise your left hand high by your left ear and prepare (5) to repeat the same sequence with your left palms, slapping (6) high and then circling clockwise (7&8) to slap low. Simultaneously, bring your right palm up near your right ear (9) to repeat the sequence again.

## SINGLE SINAWALI
### (Sticks)

When you are familiar with the single sinawali, pick up both sticks and perform the exact motions, striking the sticks together instead of your palms. (1) Assume the same ready position, right stick high near your right ear, left stick tucked underneath the right armpit pointed straight back. (2-4) Execute a high forehand strike with your right stick, then circle your stick counterclockwise for a low backhand strike while raising your left stick up high on your left side, ready to repeat the sequence with the left stick. (5&6) Execute a high forehand strike with your left stick as you tuck your right stick underneath your left armpit. Circle your left stick clockwise (7&8) to execute a low backhand strike while raising your right stick high (9) ready to repeat the sequence.

### SINGLE SINAWALI
### (Application)

(1&2) As your opponent throws a straight right punch, sidestep to your right and parry with your right hand inside his right wrist, then (3) continue circling your right arm down and back up in a counterclockwise motion, reach-

ing up for your opponent's neck or hair (4) while trapping his right arm in your right elbow. (5&6) Your opponent is off balance and easily taken down by continuing the circling motion of your right arm and pivoting your body.

## DOUBLE SINAWALI
### (Hands)

(1) Assume the same starting position as the single sinawali, with your right hand near your right ear and your left palm parallel to the ground near your waist. (2) Slap with your right palm in a high position and pull your left hand under your right armpit. Follow through by drawing your right hand toward the top of your left shoulder (3) as you slap your left palm down low. (4) Follow through again by drawing your left palm up high by your left ear and striking with your right palm in the high position. Now repeat the entire sequence only beginning with the left hand (5) slapping high, with your right hand under your left armpit, then drawing your left palm on top of your right shoulder as your right palm (6) slaps low, then (7) slap your left palm in the high position while drawing your right palm high near your right ear, (8) ready to repeat the sequence.

## DOUBLE SINAWALI
### (Sticks)

(1) Assume the same starting position as the single sinawali, with your right stick high near your right ear and your left stick tucked underneath your right armpit. (2) Execute a high forehand strike (striking your opponent's stick) with the right stick, (3) then draw your right stick to the top of your left shoulder while executing a low backhand strike with your left stick. (4) Execute a high backhand strike with your right stick and draw your left stick up high, behind your left ear, preparing to repeat the sequence on the opposite side. (5&6) Execute a high forehand strike with your left stick as you pull your right stick back under your left armpit. (7) Execute a low backhand strike with your right stick as you pull your left stick through to the top of your right shoulder. (8) Execute a high backhand strike with your left stick as you pull your right stick through and up high on your right side, (9&10) ready to repeat the sinawali. This exercise can be easily done with a one-two-three, four-five-six count in each set.

7

## DOUBLE SINAWALI
### (Application)

(1&2) As your opponent steps in with a right punch, sidestep to your left while parrying (3) his punch with your left hand, blocking from left to right. (4) Deliver a face strike with your right

hand, then grasp behind your opponent's neck (5&6) and pivot to your right on the ball of your left foot, maintaining control of his right arm and forcing him to the ground.

## REVERSE SINAWALI
### (Hands)

(1) Face your partner with your hands held up. (2) Meet your partner's right palm in a low strike while raising your left palm to your right shoulder. (3) Then bring your right palm up underneath your left armpit while striking low with your left palm. (4) Draw your left palm up near your left ear while striking low again with your right palm. (5) Strike low with your left palm while bringing your right palm to the top of your left shoulder. (6) Strike low with your right palm and bring your left palm underneath your right armpit. (7&8) Bring your right palm up high near your right ear and strike low with your left palm, completing one set and returning to the starting position. (*Note:* The last three strikes are a mirror image of the first three strikes, as in double sinawali.)

## REVERSE SINAWALI
### (Sticks)

When you are familiar with the reverse sinawali, pick up your sticks and begin (1&2) by striking low with your right stick and drawing your left stick up above your right shoulder. (3) Now execute a low backhand strike with your left stick as you follow through with your right stick by bringing it up under your left armpit. (4&5) Execute a low backhand strike with your right stick as you draw your left stick high on your left side. (6) Execute a low forehand strike with your left stick and draw your right stick back to the top of your left shoulder. (7&8) Follow through by tucking your left stick underneath your right armpit as you execute a low backhand strike with your right stick. (9) Follow through by bringing your right stick up high by your right side and execute a low backhand strike with your left stick, returning to the starting position (10) and continuing the drill.

7

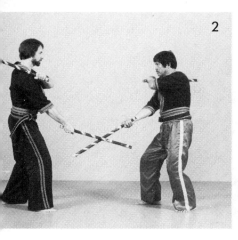

**REVERSE SINAWALI
(Application)**

(1) As your opponent attempts a right punch, (2&3) shift to your left and parry his right arm from left to right with your left hand,

slipping your right hand underneath his arm (4&5) for a groin grab. An alternate strike could be a palm strike to the neck or face.

## REDONDA
### (Twirling)

To practice this drill at first, (1) your partner should hold two sticks at a 45-degree angle on either side of his body. Starting from the sinawali ready position, pivot to the left and (2) strike down to your opponent's right stick, bring your right hand through behind your left side in a clockwise circle as your left hand comes from underneath your right armpit (3) striking your opponent's right stick backhand. Your right hand completes its circle, coming back to (4) strike the opponent's right stick one more time. Simultaneously, your left hand circles clockwise behind your left side (5) as your right hand tucks under your left armpit. Now use your left stick to deliver (6) a forehand strike to your opponent's left stick, as you pivot to the right. Follow with your right stick, (7) cutting across in a backhand motion from underneath your left armpit as your left stick circles to the right side of your body in a counterclockwise motion. As the left hand completes its circle (8) and strikes the opponent's stick, your right hand circles counterclockwise to the right side of the body. Your right hand completes its circle coming back to the starting position, (9) ready to strike the opponent's right stick as your left hand tucks under your right armpit.

2

3

5

6

8

9

## REDONDA
### (Application)

Using the motions of the first half of the redonda, a defender can block his opponent's high forehand strike (1-4) by slashing three successive strikes across the inside of his opponent's forearm (right-left-right). He can use the second half of the redonda to defend against a high backhand strike (5-8) by slashing three times across the outside of his opponent's forearm (left-right-left). Notice that the defender strikes the arm of his opponent and not the stick.

# CHAPTER 8
# Stick Disarming Techniques

**A** needed skill when dealing with any kind of weapon is knowing how to disarm your opponent swiftly. The following show 12 different disarming techniques for the 12 different strikes, but there are countless variations on these, and any may be used against more than one of the 12 strikes. Remember to practice these techniques both left- and right-handed. All of these techniques employ one stick and one free hand.

## DISARM AGAINST STRIKE #1

(1) When your opponent threatens with a high forehand strike to your head (Strike #1), sidestep to your right (2) as you execute an inside stick block and immediately grab (3) your opponent's stick in your left hand. Twist the stick quick-

ly (4-6) in a counterclockwise direction as you press
hard on his stick with your
stick, as if trying to cut it in
half. Your opponent will
either let go or be taken
down to the ground along
with his weapon.

## DISARM AGAINST STRIKE #2

(1) As your opponent attempts a high backhand strike to your head (Strike #2), sidestep to your left (2) as you execute an outside block with your stick while keeping your left hand ready to scoop (3&4) inside your opponent's right forearm. Wind your left arm

quickly in a clockwise direction until his stick is pressing against your left forearm (5) and his right wrist is pinned under your left wrist. (6) Continuing the pressure will force him to release his stick, and will keep your opponent open for a counterstrike.

## DISARM AGAINST STRIKE #3

(1) As your opponent attempts a high forehand strike to your left side (Strike #3), sidestep to your right (2) as you execute an inside block with your right stick and reach over his stick and right wrist with your left hand (3) to scoop

his wrist. (4) Wind your left arm in a counterclockwise direction (pinning his stick against your stick) and bend his right wrist backward, (5&6) forcing him to release his stick. Your opponent at this point is also off balance.

## DISARM AGAINST STRIKE #4

(1) As your opponent attempts a high backhand strike to your right side (Strike #4), sidestep (2) to your left as you execute an outside block with your right stick. (3) While keeping your left hand on his right wrist, quickly force your stick over and under-

neath your opponent's stick, raising his right wrist up (4) until your stick and your left hand are both pressing (5&6) against the back of his wrist. Force your opponent down with strong pressure until he lets go.

## DISARM AGAINST STRIKE #5

(1) As your opponent threatens with a forehand thrust to your midsection (Strike #5), sidestep to your right (2) as you execute an inside block with your stick pointed down. (3) Bring your right wrist over and outside his right wrist and your left hand up to press on his stick. (4&5) With your

4

5

right wrist and stick underneath his right wrist, pivot to your right and press against the top of his right wrist, maintaining upward pressure on the end of his stick with your left hand. (6) By swiftly pivoting to your right, your opponent's wrist will be bent backward and he will let go.

6

## DISARM AGAINST STRIKE #6

(1) Your opponent attempts a forehand thrust (Strike #6) to the left side of your body. (2) Shift to your right and block, (3) grabbing the end of his stick immediately. (4) Rotate the back end of your stick underneath

4

your opponent's right wrist and then over the top as you pivot to your right (5) forcing pressure against the back of his right wrist. (6) Follow through until he releases the stick.

5

6

## DISARM AGAINST STRIKE #7

(1) As your opponent attempts a backhand thrust to your body (Strike #7), sidestep to your left (2) as you execute a high outside block. (3) Simultaneously, reach your left hand under-

neath his right wrist and draw it quickly back (bending it at the elbow) as you press against his stick in the opposite direction with your stick. His hold will be broken.

## DISARM AGAINST STRIKE #8

(1) As your opponent threatens with a low back-hand strike to your right side (Strike #8), sidestep to your left (2) and execute a low outside block. (3) Pressing down on his stick, step in and force your right wrist inside his right arm and wind your arm upward

(4) in a clockwise circle, trapping his right wrist and stick (5) against your stick and right hand. Use your left hand to hold his stick against your own. Pivot quickly to your right (6) to bend his right wrist backward, forcing him to let go.

## DISARM AGAINST STRIKE #9

(1) As your opponent attempts a low forehand strike to your left side (Strike #9), sidestep to your right (2) as you execute a low inside block, bringing your left arm quickly to the outside of his right arm (3) to scoop his wrist. (4) Wind

your arm in a counterclock-wise direction and press against his stick with your stick. By pivoting to your right and pressing against the back of his wrist with your left hand (5&6) your opponent will be forced to let go.

## DISARM AGAINST STRIKE #10

(1) As your opponent threatens with a forehand thrust to your head (Strike #10), sidestep to your right (2) as you execute an inside block and simultaneously bring your left hand up to trap (3) his stick arm

between your left forearm and right stick. His stick is blocked against your left shoulder. (4) Pivot quickly to your right as you press downward with your left forearm, breaking his grasp on the stick.

## DISARM AGAINST STRIKE #11

(1) Your opponent attempts a backhand thrust to the right side of your body (Strike #11). (2) Shift to your left and block his stick, reaching underhand (3) to grab the end of his stick. (4) Pull his stick over the top

of your stick so that his right wrist is pulled back (5) across your stick, forcing him to release (6) his stick. Note how you have pulled his stick in a counterclockwise motion.

## DISARM AGAINST STRIKE #12

(1) Your opponent attempts an overhead strike (Strike #12) to your head. (2) Step in and block horizontally, rotating the back end of your stick around his stick to your right and then over

the top (4) of his right wrist, pulling down (5&6) on his right wrist and grabbing the end of his stick as he lets go. You are now in a position for a follow-up strike.

# CHAPTER 9

# Sword Disarming Techniques

**T**he following techniques are just a few, improvised examples of empty-hand arnis training used against attackers armed with a sword. The moves incorporate all the principles outlined in previous chapters, including body shifting, blocking-and-parrying and the circular movements characteristic of the sinawali.

These are by no means the only ways of disarming an attacker. This chapter can only give a few illustrations of how arnis empty hand moves can be applied to such situations. The multiple defenses and variations that can hypothetically be applied to other situations could easily fill an entire book.

## EXAMPLE #1

(1) As your opponent swings at your head with an overhead sword swipe, (2) execute a cross block as you shift to the side to avoid the path of his strike. Use your left forearm to block and your right forearm on top, ready to grab his wrist from the outside with your right hand. (3) Pull his sword hand high using your right hand and deliver and elbow strike (4) underneath his right armpit. (5) Pivot to your right by

stepping backward with your right foot and pivoting on your left foot. Bring your left arm up and grab his right wrist with both hands, securing the sword away from your body and pulling (6) down with both hands, setting a shoulderlock. With more pressure applied against the back of his elbow, he will drop the sword, and you can execute a takedown move from this position.

## EXAMPLE #2

(1) As your opponent threatens with a sword strike, (2) *close the distance* with your opponent by stepping in and moving to your left outside his right arm, catching the back of his right wrist in your right hand as he swings downward. (3) Step behind his right leg with your left foot and slip your left arm behind his back,

over his left shoulder and in front of his throat. Pull back hard on his right arm, straightening his elbow against your chest. (4) Using your left hand against his chin, pull back and up while maintaining a firm hold of his sword hand, and (5) execute a stomp to the back of his right knee, forcing him to collapse.

## EXAMPLE #3

(1) As your opponent threatens with an overhead sword strike, (2) close the distance as he moves in by stepping forward (in this case, with your left foot) to your left to avoid the path of his strike. At the same time, execute an upward cross block, left forearm underneath your right forearm, and use your right hand to grasp the back of his right wrist. (3) Bring your left hand up underneath his right arm and cover his right hand, trapping his hand on the sword

with both your hands. (4) Shift toward him while pulling the sword down and to your left, forcing his right arm in and the blade against his abdomen. (5) Continue turning his right wrist as you apply upward pressure against his arm, forcing the blade past his body (he may have been cut at this point). (6) Still maintaining a firm grip on his right arm, bring the sword back to your right, cutting across his abdomen again.

## EXAMPLE #4

(1) As your opponent threatens with a sword strike to your left side, (2) close the distance by stepping forward with your left foot and blocking his right arm on the inside with your left palm. (3) Follow immediately with a right palm

strike to his face, then reach your right hand back (4) behind his neck, simultaneously pushing his sword away from your body and (5) pulling his neck down into a knee strike to his face.

## EXAMPLE #5

(1) As your opponent threatens with a sword strike to your left side, (2) step forward and to your right with your right foot and block from right to left using your right hand to grab his right wrist. Simultaneously bring your left hand up outside and over his right wrist (3) and use your hips and entire body to apply downward pressure on the back of his wrist. His sword and wrist are now trapped in the crook of your elbow with the blade immobilized. (4) Maintaining a steady downward pressure with your left arm, reach up with your right hand and grab the sword from over the top, (5) shifting to your right to apply more pressure to his wrist and pulling the sword away (he has to let go or his wrist will be broken). (6&7) Now execute a downward strike against the back of his elbow (with his sword still in your right hand) to take him down.

## EXAMPLE #6

(1) As your opponent threatens with a sword strike to the left side of your body, (2) step inside his strike leading with your right foot and execute a block from right to left using your right hand against his forearm or wrist. At the same time, reach up behind his right wrist with your left hand and grab the back of his wrist. (3) Pivot immediately to your right, stepping back with your

right foot as you pull his right arm up and around with your left hand. (4) Use your left arm to twist his wrist down, forcing his palm toward you and using your whole body for leverage. (5) Trap his hand against your chest with your right hand and force your left arm against the back of his right elbow. You can now disarm him from this position and then execute a takedown.

## EXAMPLE #7

(1) As your opponent threatens with an overhead sword strike, (2) close the distance with your opponent by stepping in and to your left with your left foot and execute a palm block from left to right, deflecting his right arm to your right and grabbing (3) the back of his right wrist with your left hand. (4&5) Now pivot back to your left on your right foot, grabbing his right wrist on the inside with your right hand while continuing to cover his right hand with your left. With his hand trapped on the sword, continue pivoting back to your left as you pull his palm and wrist upward and to your left, (6&7) taking him down. (8) Maintain the twist on his wrist with your left hand and use your right hand to disarm him.